CODA: LAST POEMS

BOOKS BY KARL SHAPIRO:

Poetry:

Person, Place, and Thing
V-Letter and Other Poems
Essay on Rime
Trial of a Poet
Poems 1940-1953
Poems of a Jew
The Bourgois Poet
Selected Poems
White-Haired Lover
Adult Bookstore
Collected Poems
Love and War, Art and God
New and Selected Poems, 1940-1986
The Old Horsefly
The Wild Card: Poems Early & Late
Essay on Rime & Trial of a Poet: verse essays
Karl Shapiro: Selected Poems (edited by John Updike)

Fiction: *Edsel*

Essays:

Beyond Criticism
In Defense of Ignorance
Start with the Sun (with James E.
    Miller Jr. & Bernice Slote)
To Abolish Children
The Poetry Wreck
Creative Glut: Selected Essays

Autobiography:

The Younger Son
Reports of My Death

Libretto: *The Tenor* (opera by Hugo Weisgall)

Bibliography: *A Bibliography of Modern Prosody*

Editions:

American Poetry
A Prosody Handbook (with Robert Beum)
Prose Keys to Modern Poetry

CODA: LAST POEMS

KARL SHAPIRO

Edited and with an
Introduction by
Robert Phillips

Texas Review Press
Huntsville, Texas

FIRST EDITION, 2008

Requests for permission to reproduce material from this work should be sent to:

Permissions
Texas Review Press
English Department
Sam Houston State University
Huntsville, TX 77341-2146

Acknowledgements:

Some of these poems originally appeared in *The Texas Review* and *The Paris Review*.

Cover design by Paul Ruffin

Library of Congress Cataloging-in-Publication Data

Shapiro, Karl Jay, 1913-2000.
  Coda : last poems / Karl Shapiro.
     p. cm.
  ISBN-13: 978-1-933896-21-2 (pbk. : alk. paper)
  ISBN-10: 1-933896-21-3 (pbk. : alk. paper)
  I. Title.
  PS3537.H27C63 2008
  811'.52--dc22

                              2008005512

CODA: LAST POEMS

CONTENTS

ROSE POEMS

VARIOUS POEMS

FOREWORD

In 1983, the American poet Karl Shapiro (1913-2000) began writing a sequence of love poems to the woman who would become his third wife, the translator and editor Sophie Wilkins—just as he had written and published a book of love poems for his second wife, realtor Teri Kovach. (There is no such sequence to his first wife, Evalyn Katz, who put together and placed his first two books while he was serving in the military overseas and who was the mother of his children.)

The earlier book, *White-Haired Lover* (1968), was a celebratory cycle of twenty-nine highly personal and erotic poems. In their writing, Shapiro returned to traditional meter and rhyme, which he had abandoned in his preceding single volume, *The Bourgeois Poet* (1964). A number of the twenty-nine love poems in the present volume, *Coda: Last Poems*, also are in traditional forms, including villanelles and the sonnet. Compared to *White-Haired Lover*, they are far more tender and deeply-felt. It is clear that the poet had met the love of his life.

The existence of these poems was not known until recently. Two years after the poet's death, his wife found them in his desk in a handwritten notebook and in typescript. Nor was most of his later work generally known by the reading public. After a spat with his long-term New York publisher, Random House, Shapiro had to buy back all rights to his own poems. He then proceeded to publish new work in books that received relatively limited distribution—*Love & War, Art & God* (Stuart Wright, 1984), *Selected Poems 1940-1986* (University of Chicago Press, 1987), and *The Old Horsefly* (Northern Lights, 1992). The latter contained thirty new poems, a number of which were incisive assessments of other poets, including Ovid, Tennyson, Whitman, Eliot, Pound, Hopkins, Kunitz, Williams, Stevens, Everson, and Lowell. Other topics were Jewishness, creative writing programs, love and lust. Hardly anyone saw (or reviewed) the book.

I'm under the impression the publisher went out of business shortly after releasing the title.

In 1997, when I helped arrange for publication of the last collection published in his lifetime, *The Wild Card: Selected Poems, Early & Late* (University of Illinois Press, 1998), I asked if he had any new, unpublished poems. He said, "No." I don't know if this was a senior moment, or if he had plans to bring out the Sophie love poems separately. Stanley Kunitz and David Ignatow made the selection for that volume and did a splendid job. I was happy they included sixteen poems from the years 1969-1992, five from the obscure *The Old Horsefly*.

For this present collection, I have included just two previously published poems: "The Jewish Problem" from *The Old Horsefly*, and "Moving In" from *The Wild Card*. Both amplify themes of a number of the unpublished poems, and date from the same period.

The strongest work here, obviously, is the love poems. They celebrate the beauty of the domestic and the quotidian. It is little wonder that one of Shapiro's favorite quotations was from Walt Whitman, to the extent that one need not go hunt for beauty: "Where can you go to get away from it?" I was tempted to restrict this volume just to the love poems. They also celebrate the body parts of his beloved. An earlier poem is "The Back," in which he called that part "One of the foremost organs of beauty / Especially in women . . . ." Among the unpublished work were poems called "The Legs" and "Torso."

The flower poems are admirable as well, reminiscent of his marvelous earlier poem, "A Cut Flower," which he placed first in *Love & War, Art & God*, and which, interestingly enough, he put in the section of love poems. And even the third section, which contains some occasional poems and light verse, while admittedly not on the level of his most enduring works, reveals that Shapiro never lost his gift, his sense of humor, or his sense of indignation. He loved to tell stories on himself. During at least

one reading he read a letter he'd received from a
schoolboy. It read:

> Dear Dr. Shapiro—
> I have been assigned to write a term paper
> about you and your career, where you were
> born and educated, what kind of degrees you
> have, your rise to publications, your wife and
> children, what prizes you have won, your
> definition of poetry, and your decline. (*Reports
> of My Death*, p. 226)

These last poems show there was no real
decline. Even in his late seventies, Shapiro was
writing well.

Sophie Wilkins first met Karl Shapiro in 1942.
At the time she was married to Alvin Meyer, Shapiro's
long-time friend. Meyer had gone to medical school
in Baltimore, where Shapiro was born. Shapiro was
in uniform at the time of the meeting, about to be
shipped off to the Pacific war.

Then Wilkins' marriage to Meyer ended, and
she moved with her two sons to an apartment in
Manhattan. She had been out of touch with Shapiro
for nearly thirty years when she read an interview
with him in *American Poetry Review*. On impulse,
she wrote him. "I was feeling particularly isolated
that year, immersed since 1979 in the translation
of Robert Musil's *The Man Without Qualities* in four
volumes, for Knopf, no end in sight," she later wrote.
(*Seriously Meeting Karl Shapiro*, p. 95) That was
in August 1982. She did not know of his second
marriage, or of Teri's death in July 1982. Shapiro
came to New York in March 1983 for a week between
semesters, and they saw each other every day. The
lost had been found. She later moved to Davis,
California, where he maintained his residence.
When he retired from the University of California
at Davis later that year, he moved to her home in
New York. For some years they divided their time
between the two homes. They were married on
April 25, 1985, in Sacramento, by Judge Joseph

Decristofora. Shapiro concluded his uncollected poem, "The Dinner Party," with these lines: ". . . the new love has opened his life like a sky / From thousands of miles and forty years away."

A note on the editing: Whenever Shapiro dated his manuscripts or typescripts, I have supplied the dates. Sophie Wilkins believed most of the undated poems in the first section were written in 1984, the first year they were together. Occasionally I have corrected a spelling or added a punctuation, but largely the poems stand as Shapiro left them, in his desk drawer in uptown Manhattan, in an apartment overlooking the Cathedral Church of St. John the Divine, where his last and best Muse lived until her demise.

Robert Phillips,
Literary Executor,
The Estate of Karl Shapiro

CODA: LAST POEMS

r party for the new poet
horse, handsome and fine

it, which will go places,
his bedroom door
r-broken eyes
is no longer in his bed,
e has opened his life like a sky
miles and forty years away.

PUBLISHER ACKNOWLEDGES SPINE MISSPELLING AND REPORTS NO CORRECTION WILL BE MADE AT THIS TIME.

WAITING FOR TAKEOFF

We're next, the descending plane heaves into sight
Lights on in broad daylight
Like an iron-made moth, spread-eagled,
Pin-fixed, in rigor mortis,
Aimed right at us,
But passes over our nose as we begin
To crawl to say we're next.

The largest city goes by, with you in it.

MOVING IN

I wish you for your birthday as you are,
Inherently happy,
The little girl always shining out of your face
And the woman standing her ground.

Wish you the seldom oceanic earthquake
Which shatters your gaze
Against some previous interior past
And rights you.

Wish you your honesty normal as a tree
Confounding the caws of intellectuals.
When I zip your dress I kiss you on the neck,
A talisman in honor of your pride.

When I hold your head in my hands
It is as of the roundness of Columbus
Thinking the world, "my hands capable of
Designing the earthly sphere."

Your fingers on the piano keys
Or the typewriter keys or on my face
Write identical transcriptions.
Nothing you do is lost in translation.

I am delighted that you loathe Christmas.
I feel the same way about Communism.
Let us live in the best possible house,
Selfish and true.

May the Verdi Requiem continue to knock you out
As it does me; fashionable protest art
Continue to infuriate your heart

And make you spill your drink.

Now ideology has had its day
Nothing is more important than your birthday.
Let us have a solid roof over our head
And bless one another.

HOMEWORK

Now that I am living in your house
My highest wish is something else,
That I will make you feel at home.

Domesticity, poets say,
Blights all passions but the dollar sign,
An adage not germane to this
Undomesticatable group-of-two.

The sound of your typewriter
Is my kiss of welcome,
Your anger at tradesmen a sensual trip.

You recover quickly from the intolerable
After a silence in your oasis,
Come back with your climactic eyes,
Heat-lightning flickering still.

Journeys below are difficult for us,
Makeup, dresses, menus,
Money something we pretend to manage.

Forget but don't forget that I am here without
parole,
In love transcending hearth and home.

June 7, 1983

INTERIOR

Open my heart and you shall see
Engraved inside it—Italy!

Here in my new dwelling-place
I hang an ancient princess face
A white mask on a white wall
White on white the classic Nō
White face, black hair, black teeth
Lovely black teeth with open lips
Lipstick red, parted for speech
By ghostly lover in her plays
Through which a masculine actor speaks
And sees through old reptilian eyes
And sings and groans her tragic lines.

And just behind and underneath
A German gravure of a knight
Caparisoned and gripped by night
Holding a kind of mace upright
Going where justice says to go
And at his side a scabbard shines.

Open my heart and you shall see
(Jesus!) Japan and Germany
Lately our deadly enemy
All of us high and righteous hate
And hell-bent to exterminate
Each other's culture root and branch
G.I., samurai and mensch.

Here in this room old love has willed
To us, an amazing legacy.
May we like wordy birds rebuild
Out of the predatory past
Two lives in one that will outlast
Even the final blinding.

March 23, 1984

GERMAN

Because I love you so deeply, so shallowly,
I avoid German which I dream to learn
And know it will never happen, because you are
German,
Because I am included in you
Who are not really German but a Jew
Which is the bridge we met on after all
Over a lifetime, one of those stone rainbows
With death at both ends. I will never know
Goethe,
George, Kleist, and all that treasure, instead
I will know you, your face, your voice, your form
Informed by all the gorges and the heights
Of German, of English, of Hebrew,
The tongues of flame that surround our lives
In which we burn together
And will sleep together in each other's death.

June 7, 1983

SEA DANCE

With a glance from your sky
With the susurra of your voice
You right me.
With the kiss of the tilt of your head
With the ecliptic of your mind
You right me.
My sailor, my astronomer,
Is this what Heraclitus meant
When our souls flow into one?
With the offshore fragrance of islands
Isles sous le vent
Ilots de mémoire
All our lost years come home like treasure
Fierce and acrid as copra.
With your lift to the sun
With your threat of drowning
You right me.
And steady with glistering ropes
I will pilot to haven your riches
And anchor you to my being.

LETTER-POEM

I pen a letter to my love
who is lying in the next room
nakedly reading a poet I love whom she may not
and who welcomes my embraces
when I come to see if she is there
and opens her beauty to me,
a whole spontaneous flower to my fumbling love.

It is two months since I came to your house
and now I count the days before I go
and I am afraid.
It is your house, your city, your many years,
the whole accumulation of your life.

You have made me a room where my life takes
place,
where my writing has come to life.
To return to mindless California, what is that,
without you, what is that?

You too are afraid, afraid of your age,
afraid of your dreams, afraid I will die
from wine, from tobacco, from three-score-and-ten,
why shouldn't you be?

When my wife stopped playing the piano,
I thought she didn't love me anymore.
It was true she didn't love me anymore
and I gave up poetry.
We lived together till she died.

We have a thread between us which we dare not
break.

It is long and thin and taut,
like the string of a Stradivarius.
It stretches through forty years of our lives
and it dare not break.

You have more grace and wisdom than me,
more delicacy, more muscle.
Your beauty enthralls me when I raise my eyes.

We are foreigners, we are lovers.
We are lovers because we are foreigners.
In a sense we shall never meet.
In a sense we are husband and wife
and will die in each other's arms.

August 18, 1983

A KIND OF GIFT

I want to give you a gift
but I have to write it down.
This is not a Richard Howard poem
or an anti-poem or even a poem.
(I don't know how to buy you a ring
or a necklace or even a handkerchief.)

When Amy left the house she said,
You've given me the best gift that you can,
letting me go back to Nebraska.

We are like two batteries living
on each other's energies.
I've been living on your energy
and glow and write and charm your friends,
draining your force.

It's my turn to subside and be the battery.
I'm beginning to understand.
When we watched the sunset I took you to bed,
draining even the sunset,
and jumped back to my typewriter
all charged up.
Where did that leave you?

Come back with me to Davis if only for a day
or a week or a month or forever.
If we don't get married I understand,
if we don't go to Jerusalem I understand,
if we don't go to Vienna I understand,
or Paris or Indianapolis,
if you don't have an orgasm I understand
        all too well,

if we don't play chess I understand that too.

But in October
come hell or high water
we're going to Chicago!

April 9, 1983

A THANK-YOU

I feel you accomplished something good and right,
Easing the torque from the taut crossbow.
I'll sleep better tonight,
Sleep in the comfort of the inner glow,
Glow of your luminary love that radiates
Geographies of mistrust and gloomy states.
I feel you have accomplished lasting peace,
Tranquility domestic and heart's ease.

December 15, 1992

POEMS LIKE FLOWERS

Poems like flowers fall from my pen to you,
Poems like weeds.
Who knows the difference between flowers and
weeds?
Where is the borderline of the garden?
Whose territory is the wild?
So we cross back and forth between the tick tock
Particular of the flowerbed
And the prose poetry of the jungle scream.

July 27, 1983

THE MEANING

The quality of your beauty is unmatched
    peerless in all my life of love of beauty.
I beg you not to try to understand,
    it's better that you don't know what I
mean.

Well might you wonder why I say such things,
    pleased and suspicious at such adoration,
putting it down to poetry or wine.
    The quality of your beauty is unmatched,

peerless to one whose life has aimed at beauty,
    beauty alone unmatched in all I've seen,
peerless in all my search for beauty alone.
    I beg you not to try to understand.

The quality of your beauty is unmatched.
It's better that you don't know what I mean.

August 27, 1983

"I'LL GET BACK TO YOU"

American colloquialism

We have an endless unfinished dialogue,
Which is why I can't wait to get back to you,
Morning, evening, in my sleep.
Last night I dreamed I was waiting for the bus,
Somebody handed me a silver dollar
Which grew bigger and bigger in my hand, a-ha
George Washington's face on the coin was white
and blue
Like the flag of Israel.
George always looked like Golda Meir,
(Meyer, Meyer, Henderson and me.)

This morning you woke me, ah how you woke me,
With prosopopeia of Leslie, Hermeneutics of Lou,
And me with my hoop, chasing the ouroboros
Up slippery Broadway, into your vestibule.
Never mind this, it's only platonic foreplay
To our unfinished endless dialogue.
Though the rosebuds are showing, I'll get back to
you.

November 3, 1984

SPATE

Three nights from now, our love in spate,
Drinking the freshets of each other's faces,
Our words like bursten fountains,
Our limbs alight, our minds racing,
Poems strewn around us,
God in our genitals, our kingdom come,
Beloved, let me kiss your sleep,
Band you with touchings,
Warm you with the scintilla of afterlove,
Grapple you to my soul,
Exile forever the word goodbye.

AN EXORCISM

People with real lovers, people deeply in love,
Have imaginary lovers on the side,
A Nazi daddy, a Fascist playboy,
A side-effect of the powers thereof,
Powers that cross frontiers, language is all
nuance.
Their names appear in puns, on match boxes,
On the dust-jackets of books.
They stand in early morning dream
Watching the bed in musky dawn
When honey gathers and labiates
And succubus heaves up its flowers.

People with real lovers, people deeply in love,
Know their imaginary lovers by name
And have no shame to beckon or kiss their
photographs.
In the dawn-light of sudor nothing appalls,
The apparition says.
The apparition says, All true love is false.

February 3, 1984

First anniversary

ARCHAEOLOGY

How you collect my images, my shards—
What are these backward glances, these
immortelles?
Like everlasting photography,
That picture of me in a tent, bare to the waist,
Holding an army canteen,
Now in a rich frame on an inlaid stand
Beside the chrysanthemums—a shrine!
So you hold high the time
I buried deeper than I can dig,
Deeper than fingers of hypnosis can fathom,
Or so I thought, but am content
Not to burrow into your archivism,
Your love-dig for my images and shards.

GOD

You say I am a god.
Granted. Why beat around the bush?
Though it was only yesterday
I thought I was Caliban
which, I've been told, is an anagram
for cannibal.
But gods too are gustatory creatures.

June 26, 1983

PROPOSITION

When we're old lovers, sitting in separate chairs
Silently, will you think our love has faded
Though we smile richly and are still unaided
By doctors, accountants and presumptuous
heirs?
Though talk has frozen in geologic layers
Of long alignment of the loved and hated
And even our sexuality is jaded
And we have settled all our private cares

Including death, listen to me, adored,
Words cannot fail us ever, no matter how
The fates brighten their implements to prove
That even gods and geniuses get bored
With marriage, fucking and poetic love,
Because, beloved, we call each other thou.

LOST AND FOUND

I love to help you look for something lost,
Even a button or a mislaid book.
Sometimes it is like searching for a ghost,

And yet the searching is what matters most.
We always have to question where to look.
I love to help you look for something lost.

The missing item's what we miss the most.
Where is it hiding, in what secret nook?
Sometimes it is like searching for a ghost.

Malice of objects, goes the mystic boast,
As if the thing were something we forsook.
I love to help you look for something lost.

Where did the year go while we gaily crossed
The continent and back like jetset folk?
Sometimes it is like looking for a ghost.

Of missing time we cannot count the cost.
One year or forty's one since time awoke.
I love to help you look for something lost.
Sometimes it is like looking for a ghost.

February 18, 1989

THE BESTOWER

If there is any heaven I am in it,
The perfection of the imperfections,
The ultimate correction of the corrections.
For the first time in my life
I sleep with my door open,
Absolutely serene.
Angels and harps for Hallmark cards
Including the reproductions of masterpieces.
Wherever I see you I discover you,
On the telephone, in the kitchen, at the typewriter
With one leg cocked and your eye on the difficult
sentence,
In our bed after the movie of the poor.
I throw my heart at your feet
Simply in gratitude.
You drained the sorrow out of me like poison
And I understand the definition of fun.
Bestower, if there is any heaven I am in it,
And now there is nothing left to die.

July 10, 1983

TOTAL IMMERSION

When you burst out laughing at me
and cover your face with your hands
like a little girl,
I am unaccountably flooded with happiness,
a total immersion in an ecstasy
that has no name. Nor do I pretend to know
what you are laughing about.
And do not even wish to inquire,
but wait to surface from your light-heavy waves
to clasp you dropping in my arms.

July 26, 1983

TORSO

This little torso of yourself you carved
Is now my talisman and apt to be
My god, so much I cherish it,
Fondle it, squeeze, consult it with my lips.
It darkens under my kiss,
It fits my hand as you fit me
In the numinous magic of metting,
Your graven image indistinguishable
From the giant original.

Absent from you I kiss
Your breasts the size of seedless grapes,
Swell of your belly, beauty mark of navel,
Parnassus of mons veneris, rise of thighs,
Cut off at the rough honeycomb of wood.

The back exquisite as a river valley
Rising to buttes, the separate curve of hams.
Blessed carving, loving toy,
I all but eat you, a delicious feast.
Which one you are I cannot tell,
You do yourself so well,
The magiscule, the miniscule.
I say your name till I'm unmanned.
I write this poem with you in hand.

Oct. 1, 1984

TORSO FETISH

> **Shall I fall down before a block of wood?**
> —THE TALMUD

As Buddhists thumb their beads
As Romans kiss the toes
Of Michaelangelo's
Pieta, or they did
Before the vandal struck,
I thumb your figurine
For love and for good luck
And satisfy my needs
Superego and id
Both sacred and obscene.

Mysterious that my lips
Feel so at home to rest
Upon this tiny breast
Which Lawrence called his home,
The bosoms of his wife
Abundantly endowed,
His Sweet retreat from strife
To love's apocalypse
Where beauty is to come
And no limb disallowed.

The wandering spirit seeks
And finds its talisman
To domicile within.
You have entered yourself alone
And handed yourself to me
To cherish with all my flesh.

O weird idolatry
As pagan as the Greeks

I stroke your image and moan
And fall upon you afresh.

January 31, 1984

THE LEGS

In the summery room I look up from writing
Stunned at the sight of your legs
Color of travertine
Soft marble of villas, a waterstone
Warm and cool to the hand porous
With a suggestion of apenine blue
Exceptionally nude almost translucent
So that the sinews flicker like saplings
With vertical rills like dorian fluting,
Witness the curve of the calf
In its rise to the knee-socket
The complicated frown of knee
Upon which stands more wrought than Grecian urns
The sculpture of thigh
Glory of the handlers of the stuff of gods
And goddesses
Where graze my fingertips like sheep
My lips nibble like lambs
And my tongue drinks in the deepest of thirsts
From the proud fountain of your definition.

July 1, 1983

THE WALK-THROUGH

Walk through the city of power, poet and lover,
Licking up glances of envy, delight, and dismay,
Seeing, unseeing, up to the utmost tower,
Concentrating the world in your swollen hearts,
Your swimming eyes, your virginiality, old lovers.

All grace you are, no need to concentrate,
People part from you on the sidewalk,
Reel away from the manifest happiness.
Muggers won't mug you, Pneumococcus sleeps,
Cars drive around your particular magic,
Your names are inscribed in future anthologies.

March 11, 1983

TALISMAN

It's in your provenance I would be
      as a work of art.
It's in your governance I would be
      a province of your heart.

A set-designer of the sky
Rolls out a cloud, a brilliant piece of dark.
Time clicks a cliché.
"Spring is coming."
But there's the continental divide.
My airplane climbs the seven-mile mountain
In the wrong direction.
I fly against the sun.

I'm going home to help the equinox,
Talk through the ether, wait
Until I feel your breasts against my breast
This second spring.

December 20, 1983

NO DOUBT

Against your own judgment, in a fit of self-doubt
You denigrate your looks, using criteria
You wouldn't use for poets or for maenads.
Thank God you don't look like Marilyn Monroe.
Models never gave me an erection,
Or even made me turn my head one inch.
I don't understand those armatures called
models.
Models of what?

Without our defects we would be dummies;
The defects are incorporate in beauty;
Vaunted perfection is a scam.
When you come to me without preparation,
My love pounds harder than pile-drivers.

I will paint you on the very Ark
Where the overdressed torahs are snoozing
inside.
For you I stand up, for you I doven,
Bobbing up and down like a cork in the Baltic.

And please don't think you are in the eye-of-the-
beholder
Or any of those highsounding platitudes.
But come to me in your blakean swiftness
Like a ray from a comet.

THE SPEAR

Be good to my Love!
Watch him for me!
Take care of him for me!
　　　　—SOPHIE

Your cry, your prayer transfixes me
Not with the beesting of the wingéd boy,
Not with the fleche d'amour,
But with a spear between my ribs
That splits me through the heart.
Your aim is fast and true,
Your shaft impales me.

I met a gardener in the supermarket
Who said, Long time no see,
A big man, a sweet man
Who tends the exotic campus trees,
The cork oak and the olive and the fig.
We always chatted across his wheelbarrow.
He had almost died from a heart attack,
Said he was fine, his wife said he was fine.
They split him open and mended his heart.
The checker computed my cheese and wine
And said, Have a nice day.

Be good to my beloved's eyes,
Watch her for me,
Take care of her for me.

January 29, 1984

RIGHTS

I have no rights over you, my own,
No right to say "my own,"
I don't own you. Nobody does,
Especially the unknowable you.
It may be I please you too much,
Frightening your singular self,
My Austrian, American Jew,
What right have I to say, "my"?
Your time, your childhood, your future,
Are not my property.
How shall we live together?
We tell each other we are synonymous,
While I fill your house with smoke,
While I drink a liter of wine,
While you turn me into a prince with your hands,
While I worship your body, down to the quick.
I respond like a boy.
And you accept it, you accept it all,
And turn it all in my favor,
And I accept your acceptance.
But I am afraid.
I am afraid it is not enough.
I am afraid I jumped out of a letter
And stood before you like an afreet.
I am afraid you think you invented me,
That you won me in a lottery and wish
You hadn't read the paper that day.
I am afraid you would rather go back to your
owness
Among your corridors of books, your reels
Of phonecalls, your ecloguic letters,
My letters among them, which woke me

From my moribund resignation.
No, I am not afraid you don't love me
Synonymously with my love for you.
It's obvious we are inseparables.
It's obvious that we have closed the door
Behind us. Even if you left me without a look,
Even if I left you without a look,
Even if one of us died,
Already we have fulfilled each other
And we have barely begun to meet.
When you walk past me, you take my breath
away.
I'm foolish enough to be jealous
If you chat with the grocer.
But what's so foolish about love?
I know we have rights in each other,
As if we'd been married for a century,
Already an inarticulate understanding
Which looks like ennui to strangers.
And in your world which I am invading,
As in my world that you have conquered,
Remember that we have interchanged lives
And that, for better or for worse,
There cannot be any longer
Any poetry of departure for us.

ROSE POEMS

LATE BLOOMER

There always seems to be another rose
Even in January under the white-gold sky,
Though you're not there among the bushes,
Clippers in hand, risking the thorns.
I picked a pink one yesterday
And peeled three mildewed petals off,
Exposing a beauty almost shamelessly
With that pure fragrance of your skin.
Now the deciduous trees are naked,
A few pomegranates are hanging leathery,
Some oranges are dropping of their weight
And the pool is full of leaves.
Everything is in a waiting period.
My dreams are peculiar, even the telephone waits
And already this morning
The rose flew open like a cyclamen.

Feb. 1, 1984

HOTHOUSE FLOWER

Forced flower, hasty rose, where did you come from?
What borough birthed you under the milky panes?
Beautiful you are, commercial flower,
Frigid-perfect, with no blemishes,
Though lacking in scent, compared with your
natural sisters,
But is anything natural anymore?

April 7, 1984

HARVEST

Red rose, six feet tall,
It is the leggy time of year.
Red rose, proud in September,
Proud as a symbol, stay where you are.

Now is the wine-grape harvest,
Now is the crushing time of year
On the slopes of the vineyards.
The narrow roads are jammed with trucks
Moving the harvest.
The "cellar rats" are rolling their barrels.

Red rose, six feet tall,
It is almost time for the pruning shears.

September 23, 1987

PREPOSITIONS

These roses are to make love by,
Love under and to make love to,
To kiss your body while I kiss you.
O lovely Sonya, pink as leaping fish,
How mouth your namesake openly,
Unfolding lips within the heavenly hell,
An insideout volcano down your slopes
Intrinsic as the earth since Adam fell.

Dec. 15, 1983

VASE OF DEAD ROSES

Even the petals of the surrounding succulents
Jaundice and fall,
Fern stiffens to primness and leafage crinkles and
falls
Dry as potato chips,
But the roses, Sonyas by name, look hanged,
Faces straight down, as if their necks were
broken,
Drooping earthward, twelve silent bells
After their clock has struck.

When I start to remove them you say,
They are still beautiful, let's leave them there.

VARIOUS POEMS

THE DAY THAT PAINTING DIED

for Joseph Niépce, 1826

On that day in 1826
When the first photo saw the light of day,
(Only a couple of roofs and a possible tree,)
painting died.

People began to walk off the canvas,
Landscape became a lovely blur,
Bone turned its back on flesh,
Skeleton was king,
Till skeleton itself began to shrink.

Nothing remained on canvas except idea,
Blank canvas thinking what to think.

Into this vacuum stepped the photograph.
Everyman had a camera eye,
Everyman became artist,
Every album a personal Louvre,
Till ultimately, inevitably,
Photo began to live and breathe,
Photo began to move and laugh,
Photo began to kiss and kill.

Crowds in the darkness worhipped at the light,
Wallpaper swallowed women,
Tables broke their backs and legs,
Gods and gangsters and giant girls
Hung there on the velvet wall,
Hung there like a shot guitar,
And hung there like a Rothko at the Tate,
The day that painting died.

August 30, 1992

THE CAMERA

The camera was a failure, wasn't it?
It failed in modeling, it failed in expression,
The brilliant background darkened,
Light overshadowed character lines,
Eyes changed color,
And worst of all, feeling was cancelled out.

This voyeur, this machine,
Perfectly programmed to its Me,
Isn't much help, this idiot savant
Is not an extension of ourselves at all,
But a cold cave wherein
Ignorant shadows bump and curse and kill
As in a blacked-out subway hell.

June 25, 1983

BALLPOINT PENS

Ballpoint pens are dead except they work.
Except they work the ball there is no point
To mate the paper of the average jerk
And poets whose juncture is the ballpoint joint.

All citizens, abandon ballpoint ink!
It eats the paper through in one decade,
Erases every thought that you can think
And leaves lace-paper in the poem you made.

Poets of ages past, holy of holies,
How come our poems have all turned into doilies?

THE SACRED BLUE

They say the Greeks, who had a word or
everything,
Had no word for blue.
Some even thought they could not see blue,
The people of the wine-dark sea,
The people of the murex,
Noble purple denied to all by nobles.
Aristotle saw only three colors in the rainbow,
And none were blue.
Does blue belong to a higher consciousness?
Is blue of a higher sky,
Higher even than Plato thought?
Blue of Israel, blue of Mary's color,
The sacred blue.

December 16, 1992

LANDSCAPE

Twice as high as the beautiful street standard
Rise the fresh Canary Island pines,
    Softly conversing.
Far to the southwest marches a cloud-wall
    Tainted with smog.

1988

I DECLARE PEACE

I declare peace.
Peace to the shadowy man with the knife
Peace to the spires spikey green
Peace to the bonded brickwork, the crack in the
marble
Peace to the sky that tries to be blue but settles
for gray
Peace to the potted tree safe from the droppings
of dogs
Peace on concrete, peace on the whiskey building
On vegetarians and hogwallowers
On missile-minders, on priests smaller than
insects
          under the upswooping nave
On rabbis fuming in their soup
Peace on all that.

Nature that minds not, go thy ways,
For what we declare will make no difference
Either to David Rex or to the salt-tax.
Peace on our synonymity
Peace on our peace.

1983 or 1984

THE SOLDIER

all evil shed away
  —Rupert Brooke

Establishing the flag upon a rock
Or running from his running blood
Or laced in cords of silk and shod in nails,
His hand kissing the instep of his gun,
Riding the bloodstream of the populace
Down boulevards that surge like tapestries
—He passes to the stock response of peace.

But observe the professional soldier, forty-odd,
Perched on the tube edge of a perfect cot,
With eyes unshut, thin, hard as a knot,
A whited buddha, in pure underwear,
The absolute domestic. The raw floor
Scrubbed to the grain, leaks acid on the air;
His nostrils flare, and smoke leaks round his
teeth.

This is the man who makes the bed,
This is the man with the faceless face
Who tries to put back something in its place
That is already in place, who can be free
Only inside the nail-bright cell.
The points of darkness stream into his eyes.
This is the man of peace, who holds
No other image in his soul than peace
—Who passes to the stock response of war.

AFTER THE SURRENDER

After the surrender
When hundreds of thousands of Americans
Flew and drove and walked all over Japan
General McArthur issued an order

—Any American who slaps a Japanese
    Will be given five years in the penitentiary—

A Japanese general wrote in his diary:
"It was then I knew we had lost the war."

March 4, 1987

TRAJECTORY

It is like the dream of the soldier coming home
Vectoring away from the horror, reprieved from death,
To be coming to her
Hurtling above the fleshy curve of earth
Descending with a roar in his arteries
Anonymous, without fanfare,
To search the stare of faces for her face
Beyond the check-points, into the alien crowd,
To clasp the one synonymous life.

1983

FEMINIST POEM

I would like to write a feminist poem
But I love women, woman *qua* woman,
     if you know what I mean.
If you're a feminist, you don't.
I'd like to write a feminist poem
That opens the door to the lady in woman,
But these days you'd better think twice
Before you open any door
To what seems to be
a female of the species.

PROVERBS

Religions are evil, all of them, and inevitable.
But religion is natural and holy.
It takes a brush to clean a comb,
A comb to clean a brush.
The singular is abstract, plural concrete,
God thinks in particulars: e.g.,
No two of anything is alike.
But rubrics pressure the sanity of chaos.
All wary are wary of religions
And there is no such thing as peace.
Peace is a time to clean the bore of your rifle.
The atheist is the religion of all.
Beware the blue eye of the idealist.
Man is a mud pie.
The state is a gigantic ear,
Even music cannot escape the censor.
Flags are the blood of nations let loose.

THE TENSES

Women live in the past.
They are a separate caste.
Men live in the future,
It's their nature.
Children (and poets) live in the present.
The banging of their highchairs is incessant.
God lives in all the tenses,
And many that are far beyond our senses.

SECOND OPINION

for Dr. Janet Slavitt,
with thanks

I got a second opinion,
Thinking the first was a myth,
But I didn't like that one either,
So I got a third and a fourth and a fifth.
Then it suddenly dawned on me,
This is just a conspiracy
To resurrect phlebotomy.
How much of my blood? I hear
Ninety-six gallons a year!
Dumped in the river, all mine.
The multitudinous seas incarnadine.

AN APOLOGY TO A BULLDOG

Since even dogs can read American,
According to Miss Moore, I hope, Margo,
That you will at your ease presume to scan
This apologia from a Clumsy Toe
That came down on your foot on Thursday night.
This you announced with an indignant yelp.
I thank the Lord you didn't take a bite
Out of my calf and make me yell for help.
My sole was rubber I am glad to say,
Or you just might have used those curvy fangs
That overlap your lip and cause dismay
To friend and burglar and even to street gangs.
However, I don't mean to invade your Id;
I'm only sorry that you went and hid.

October 5, 1990

KARL SHAPIRO

to Saul Bellow

But as for K, I, lover of K,
(Be upstanding, Karl!)
Even as a child I felt the weakness of C,
A giving-in, a curvature of the spine.
K was like my atheist German grandfather
I never knew, and so I switched to K,
But now immortalized by the great K of Prague.

But Saul, who is your Shapiro character?
Some nebbich, some McCullough of the mind?
In New York Shapiro is a specific for Smith,
A Jewish John, a Doe, a non.
In California they think it is Italian,
Spire and Schiaparelli are redactions.
Now I see Shapiro poets all over the map,
Upstarts trading on my moniker,
None of them special,
My non-name, a forgotten pause
Buried in some Bavarian almanack.

BAR MITZVAH

—for Matthew

A hail of hard candies
rattled down on the dais
when the boy was pronounced a man.
Huckleberry Finn, son of a Jewish mother
a WASP father dead in a car crash
and foster-fathered by extension
of the family as we grow it
via death, divorce, regroupings,
by an Orthodox computer scientist
and a Norse healthscape architect,
voted his Jewish heritage in and
learned Hebrew for his bar mitzvah.
Why, we asked him, choose to be a Jew?
He said he saw it was a way to learn a lot!
And so his bar mitzvah was held
in Oakland, California, that place
where there's no there there, avant-garde
Place Without Qualities, in a lighter-than-air
pavilion, afloat on sunkissed greenery
in a belt of windows, and a hundred friends came.
The chassidic rabbi led the chanters
between the blessings read out in Hebrew
brought out of the closet and worn by the
honored few
like a talliss and t'fillim, with awed formality.
The apple-faced candidate for manhood
bent over the 600-years-old scroll
somehow rescued from the German holocaust
and smoothly read those oriental letters
inscribed on the huge roll of parchment
by a medieval hand, in an earlier catastrophic
time,

the fourteenth century of our Christian era.
He read those sensuous curling flames of holiness
scimitar flourishes of homage to the everliving
tree of life and wit, then gave his own
explication de texte on the theme of Jacob and
Esau
on that perennial war between brothers
which is the making of history: Why
Cain and Abel, Isaac and Ishmael, Jacob and
Esau?
Is there no other way?
Must brother always cheat, kill drive out
his brother, for the blessing always
and forever midwifed by a curse?
It is God's will, our reader concluded.
That's a cop-out, said the Devil, God's house
critic
(who always gets the best lines, if not always the
last word),
who bides his time and plots his courses
whereby the various degrees of manhood
are climbed like Everest, because they are there.
Suddenly at the peak of this Old Testament
high tension, the kids in the ad hoc congregation,
who had sat so still for so much ritual,
pelted the new bridegroom of the Shekhinah
with hard candies hurtling at him like buckshot:
baptism by fire of sweets. He was sucking one
before the rabbi had got to his final Amen.

THE JEWISH PROBLEM

for Stanley Burnshaw

Every Jew has a Jewish problem, namely,
If you are a Jew and you're not paranoid, you're
crazy.
Freud had the Jewish problem in spades,
Marx was the Typhoid Mary of the Jewish
problem,
   The grandpa of the Holocaust.
I once met a forester in California and I thought
right off,
This fellow doesn't have a Jewish problem.

People ask me, Have you been to Israel?
I answer No, and I have no intention of going.
This is a new Jewish problem.

I once published a book called Poems of a Jew,
To get rid of my Jewish problem.
It only made it worse.

When people ask me about the Holocaust
I say, Tell it to Germany.

When the sun is over the yard-arm and I mix my
gin martini,
Or pour a glass of ruby Côte du Rhône,
I always say Boyray pree ha gophen,

Achtung! Greek or Roman Christian,
Baptist holy-roller in the dust,
Stop calling me Jew.

Achtung! Sunni or Shiite Moslem,

Fondling your pineapple hand grenade,
Stop calling me Jew.

Achtung! Israeli or American,
Orthodox conservative or reform,
Stop calling me Jew.

Listen to me, believers of the faiths, this is my
song:
America is Israel, nor am I out of it.

February 17, 1990

UBI SUNT

Marilyn had baby flesh
The kind that won't hold up.
In a bad sonnet I wrote a good line
About her cold lewd lips.

Dorothy had breasts as hard as baseballs
With witch-hairs on her nipples.

Jenny seduced me where I sat
Recoiling on her wide divan
Till I was spent.
It was her daughter that I meant
Down in the cellar at the ironing-board.

Joyce's bosom was Junoesque.
I don't remember that she moved her hips.
Once when I screwed her she was eating an
apple.

Joan always ready, Joan always wet,
Moaned like an Eskimo,
Her cunt was sweet as pears to eat.

Lola's nipples popped out like doorbells.

Paula had the feel of a platinum watch.

Phyllis exuded a delicate sweat
And had studied fucking in Paris and Carthage.

Elaine lay like a lily and was loved.

The Polish woman was a movie beauty

With one inverted nipple (she announced)
And a noble ass. She asked to be beaten.

Black-Irish beautiful Sue had no breasts,
Kept her brassiere on and was tight as a virgin
That one time.

Madelaine came to my office with no pants
And raised her tight skirt navel high.

Karen holed up in the Cornhusker Hotel
For three days while I came and went.
In the midst of a plunge she said to me,
Ginsberg says you can't write for shit.

Bea was built like a man with buttocks of granite.
Taught me buggery till her husband caught us.
She passed me to Hulga, whose bedroom was red.
Her husband took my picture for a jacket cover.
I am smoking a pipe.

Laid by her father, deep-voiced Donna
Frigged herself with a waxed cucumber,
Locked my head between her spastic thighs,
Drank gin by the quart and lectured on Faulkner.

In steaming Calcutta, bedridden, exhausted by
Hinus,
I went down on Agnes, her Sexual Preference.
She followed me home to San Francisco.

Through the skirts of the hurricane Freya raced
And leapt on me in the guestroom bed,
Raping and pillaging while she bled.
Morning the sheets were drenched with red.

On State Department trips to Europe
I remained faithful, afraid to get caught,
Except for one magnificent whore in Hamburg,
And with her I failed to get an erection
And was scolded in German.

Stayed faithful to Frances for fifteen years,
Though sex had long since flown out the window.
I once found black panties on the floor of the car
And handed them to her, no questions asked.

TWELVE MALEDICTIONS

1.

I wish we could form a posse to hunt down
        the sonofabitch who invented the
expression
        The American Dream
And spool out his large intestine, the way our
Native American sqaws were taught, and feed
the live intestine to the dogs.

2.

I wish we could catch the cocksucker
Masculine, feminine, or neuter
Who forever crucified the beautiful-
        gentle-irreplaceable
        adjective-transexualized-to-noun-
        puckish-multi-faceted jewel-of-a-word—
        Gay
And make him chew up and swallow
        the whole thirteen volumes of the OED
        plus the Supplements until he bowelled
out.

3.

Somewhere over the rainbow there must be a poet
        with crossbow and arrows tipped with
cyanide
        to split the breastbone and aorta of the
lexical savage

who invented as a mark of punctuation
the sweet and subtle adverb
Hopefully
And let's ship to San Quentin for an
indeterminate lockdown
whoever mouths Hopefully at the beginning
of a sentence.

4.

May a hell of head lice, blueballs, putridity and
Parkinson's
overtake the euphuistic rat who first
vomited
the unspeakable metonymy
Senior Citizen
May he be run over by an electronic wheelchair
And brained by a crutch.

5.

But pity those well-uniformed well-paid wage-
slaves
at the checkout counter who are instructed
to say
with a smile, Have a Nice Day,
which somehow, unlike Grüss Gott or Thank You,
comes off
as an insult.

6.

Chain-shot for those who use impact as a verb,

Update as an hour-mark, and data base as
a come-on.
May green light melt down and dissolve their
eyeballs.

7.

May they contract AIDS from a pay toilet
   who use minority to designate
a single separate person.

8.

May a sudden and swift case of Downs Syndrome
sink into the central nervous system
of the sociologist-rhetorician who coined
in a dark hour the snide and cynical expletive
   the Third World.

9.

May they be imprisoned in a colony of hare-lips
who use the ancient and elegant criteria
in the singular.

10.

And for those who use media as the singular
with an article, ditto.

11.

May all these imprecations and then some
    crash down on the plotters and planners
    who fishing in a befoulment of culture and
sub-culture
    dragged up through the wriggling slime
the barbarous and illiterate Ms.—
once the honorable decoction of manuscript
and now gyno-political cock-trap.

12.

Language of course is always in flux,
now like a cleanly river, now like a white water
rapids
    Now like a freshet, now like a waterfall
    Now like a lake or a pond
Now like a sink, now like a cesspool.

AGAIN, FOR SOPHIE

Roses in late November
Here where the skies begin
Bring poetry back to love.
Thank you for bringing them in.

ABOUT THE AUTHOR

Karl Shapiro (1913-2000) was one of the most distinguished poets of America's Middle Generation, the generation of Lowell, Berryman, Schwartz, Roethke and Bishop. Shapiro's second poetry collection, *V-Letter and other Poems*, was awarded the Pulitzer Prize in 1945 when he was thirty-two. In 1946 he was appointed Consultant in Poetry at the Library of Congress, the position now called U.S. Poet Laureate. From 1950 to 1956 he was editor of *Poetry: A Magazine of Verse*, and from 1956 to 1966 he edited the quarterly *Prairie Schooner*. He was awarded the Bollingen Prize in Poetry in 1969 "for the continuing achievement represented in *Selected Poems*," published the previous year. He taught at Johns Hopkins University, the University of Nebraska, the University of Illinois at Chicago, and the University of California at Davis, from which he retired. Shapiro was a member of the American Academy of Arts and Letters and spent his last years in Manhattan. He was subject of the film, *Karl Shapiro's America*.